Images of War
Victory in Europe

RARE PHOTOGRAPHS FROM WARTIME ARCHIVES

Andrew Rawson

Pen & Sword
MILITARY

First published in Great Britain in 2005 by
PEN & SWORD MILITARY
an imprint of
Pen & Sword Books Ltd,
47 Church Street, Barnsley,
South Yorkshire.
S70 2AS

ISBN 1-84415-274-X

A CIP catalogue record for this book is available from the
British Library

Printed and bound in Great Britain by CPI UK

Many of the photographs in this book have been reproduced
with kind permission of the United States National Archives.
Captions indicate the photograph reference number.

Pen & Sword Books Ltd incorporates the imprints of
Pen & Sword Aviation, Pen & Sword Maritime, Pen & Sword
Military,
Wharncliffe Local History, Pen & Sword Select,
Pen & Sword Military Classics and Leo Cooper.

For a complete list of Pen & Sword titles please contact:
PEN & SWORD BOOKS LIMITED
47 Church Street, Barnsley, South Yorkshire, S70 2AS, England.
E-mail: enquiries@pen-and-sword.co.uk
Website: www.pen-and-sword.co.uk

Contents

Introduction

By January 1945, Allied troops had been in northwest Europe for over six months. After heavy fighting in Normandy, General Eisenhower's Armies had broken out and advanced rapidly to the German border, liberating Paris and Brussels. Another Allied landing in southern France swept up the Rhone Valley, joining the main drive to the German border. However, by the end of September, the advances started to falter, not through enemy action but mounting difficulties in keeping the front line troops supplied. As summer turned to autumn, an attempt to cross the Rhine at Arnhem using airborne troops, codenamed Operation Market Garden, ended in failure and Eisenhower was forced to reconsider his options.

Hard fighting followed as the Germans regrouped and bitter battles for Aachen, the first German city to fall, and Hurtgen Forest consumed men and supplies alike. On 16 December 1944 the Germans struck back with two Panzer Armies in the Ardennes, breaking through the American lines and threatening to reach the River Meuse. For two weeks American reserves poured into Belgium as rearguards fought to hold vital crossroads at St Vith and Bastogne to hold back the German onslaught and by the beginning of January the tide was beginning to turn. The worst was over and as American and British troops squeezed the Bulge out of the Allied line, Eisenhower was planning to strike deep into Germany.

By the beginning of January the Allies had seventy-one divisions ready for action and another fourteen were due to land on the continent over the weeks that followed. Meanwhile, the attack in the Ardennes had consumed a large part of Hitler's reserve. With the Allies poised on the borders in the west and the Russians threatening to carve across eastern Germany it was only a matter of time before Hitler's thousand year Reich came to an end.

Eisenhower had six Armies facing the Germans along a broad front with a vast logistical organisation poised for the final push by the start of the New Year and would start by clearing troops from the Siegfried Line and the west bank of the Rhine. Field Marshal Montgomery's 21 Army Group would then cross the river between Emmerich and Wesel, north of the Ruhr, and drive into northern Germany while General Omar Bradley's 12 Army Group bridged the river between Mainz and Karlsruhe in the south. Having broken Germany's last barrier, the stage would be set for the final drive into the heart of Germany, with the centres of industry, the Ruhr and the Saar basin, the primary objectives.

The end of the war and Victory in Europe was in sight but there was hard fighting ahead. Hitler and the Nazis had motivated the entire German population to fight the invaders and the Allied soldiers would have to fight every inch of the way.

Chapter One

February 1945
Breaking the Siegfried Line

BY MID-DECEMBER 1944 the Allied Armies were poised to strike into the heart of Germany having endured a gruelling autumn campaign. As Eisenhower considered his next move Hitler struck back in the Ardennes with all the armoured reserves he could muster in what would be known as the Battle of the Bulge. With surprise on their side two Panzer Armies ripped through the thin American line in a few days and threatened to cross the Meuse River and split the Allied line in two. A combination of heroic defensive actions at places such as St Vith and Bastogne and bad weather stalled the German advance long enough to allow the Allies to gather their own reserves and contain Hitler's armour. After two weeks, the crisis had passed and the German troops found themselves on the defensive in a deadly salient. By the end of January the Bulge had been eradicated and once again the Allies were able to plan their campaign to defeat Germany.

Field Marshal Montgomery discusses the forthcoming battles with his American allies.

With seventy-one divisions available and another fourteen due in the spring, Eisenhower's first objective was to destroy the German forces west of the Rhine. The first strike came in the north in 21 Army Group's sector and on 8 February the First Canadian Army launched Operation VERITABLE. For two weeks General Crerar's men endured harsh weather conditions and heavy resistance as they pushed southeast from Nijmegen and the Reichswald Forest towards the Rhine.

21 Army Group's second attack, in Ninth US Army's sector, was scheduled to start at the same time, driving northeast to link up with the Canadians and encircle German forces trapped on the west bank. However, before General Simpson's men could cross the Roer River, a series of dams controlling the flow of water had to be taken. V Corps struck out through the Hurtgen Forest, scene of bitter fighting the previous autumn, on 5 February and five days later seized the key Schwammenauel Dam before German engineers could destroy it. They had, however, damaged valves controlling the flow of water, delaying Simpson's attack until the floodwaters had subsided.

In 12 Army Group's sector General Omar Bradley made limited advances and by the end of February his troops had broken through the Siegfried Line between Pruem and Saarburg and he was ready to make his own drive to the Rhine. On the southern end of the Allied line General Jacob Devers' 6 Army Group concentrated on straightening the line and by 9 February the Seventh US Army and the First French Army had cleared the German salient known as the Colmar Pocket and were ready to advance towards the Rhine.

After reducing the Bulge in the American line, General Bradley continued his offensive in the hope of pushing the Germans back towards the Kyll River. This antitank crew of 345th Regiment have set up their weapon alongside a wayside shrine in Schonberg, Belgium during 87th Division's attack on Neuendorf.   111-SC-199957

(Right) A wounded Tommy is attended by stretcher bearers. He and his pal were hit during heavy fighting – his friend is dead. Stretcher bearers have stuck their flags into the ground to show the enemy that they are attending a wounded man. The Germans defending the position have just surrendered and are being escorted to the rear.

While 21 Army Group made the main Allied effort in the north, Third Army spent February battling its way through the Siegfried Line, between Pruem and Saarburg and by the end of the month had captured the Orscholz Switch Line, the Saar-Moselle triangle, and the city of Trier. These infantrymen of the 94th Division run for cover as shells rain down on Sinz.
111-SC-200243

British infantrymen drive the enemy out of a village in Second British Army's sector.

Although the Allies held the advantage, attacking the German lines at will, local commanders did their up most to stall the advance with local counterattacks. After reports of enemy troops massing opposite his front Major-General Harry Malony has called up the reserves of the 94th *Neuf-Cats* Division to shore up the line near Sinz in the Saar-Moselle Triangle.
111-SC-200180

Private Ausman loops a noose around the neck of his Hitler effigy on the Patton Bridge over the River Sauer. General Patton commented that he had never seen such a group of small men building such a large bridge and the nickname the Mighty Midgets stuck.
111-SC-200993

Private Ray David inspects an armour-plated turret overlooking the Sauer River near Echternach on the German border. Armour-piercing shells failed to penetrate the ten-inch thick steel plate but this, and other equally formidable fortifications, did not stop the 76th *Onaway* Division smashing through the Siegfried Line en route to the Prum River.
111-SC-200702

Company E of 358th Regiment passes through a line of fortifications in the Siegried Line during 90th Division's drive to the Prum River. Rows of concrete obstacles known as Dragon's Teeth, barbed wire, pillboxes and minefields were supposed to halt Third Army's advance; they failed.
111-SC-200383

Tough Ombre Private George Beaver fires his .30 calibre machinegun at a German position during 90th Division's attack on the Siegfried Line near Habschied. Private John Ward shouts directions to the gunner while Private James Cappo keeps the gun well supplied with belts of ammunition.
111-SC-200263

Despite heavy losses in men and materials during the Ardennes Offensive, the German resolve stiffened as soon as the Allies crossed the border and casualties began to mount as Hitler urged his troops to fight for every inch of the Fatherland. These medics are busy strapping a wounded man to the stretcher on their jeep as his comrades look on anxiously.
111-SC-200245

'General Mud', was the chief opponent during the February offensives, restricting movement to major roads as rivers flooded and fields disappeared beneath a sea of mud. The driver of this lorry is struggling to coax his vehicle forward as he makes his way towards the Our River in Belgium.
111-SC-200084

The constant movement of traffic quickly transformed all but the main highways into quagmires. The crew of this self-propelled 155mm howitzer is struggling to reach its assigned position as 737th Tank Battalion prepares to support 5th Division's attack on the Siegfried Line. 111-SC-200260

A Churchill flame-thrower tank (Crocodile) clears the way for British infantry.

The men suffered and regular supplies of hot food and dry clothing were essential to keep their spirits up. This medic enjoys a warm meal before returning to the front line.

After spending nights sleeping in muddy foxholes during the battle for the Prum sector of the Siegfried Line these GIs from the 4th Division make the most of their cold K-Rations before settling down for the night in a German pillbox. 111-SC-201205

A M10 Hellcat of 803rd Tank Destroyer Battalion fires its 76mm gun at a German pillbox in Ecternach, Luxembourg. The tank destroyer is supporting 5th Division's drive across the Sauer River as General Patton's Third Army advanced towards the Siegfried Line. 111-SC-200040

As the Germans were forced back across their border they took steps to hinder the Allied advance. Private Leroy Blanchard of the 11th Armoured Division has discovered a Panzerschreck leaning suspiciously against a wall and has rigged up a piece of cord to test it for booby-traps rather than move it by hand. 111-SC-200081

As the Germans withdrew, large quantities of arms and ammunition fell into Allied hands. Here Privates Kulmer, Totsky and Rouse are looking forward to testing these machine-guns in case they ever need to rely on captured weapons. 111-SC-199967

The Ardennes offensive in December 1944 had seriously depleted German armoured reserves and by the following spring they were using every available vehicle to stem the Allied attacks. This American armoured car had been captured during the Battle of the Bulge and served its captors for two months before it was knocked out by artillery fire. III-SC-299955

4th *Ivy* Division cleared the town of Prum, during Third Army's attack on the Siegfried Line. These GIs are taking no chances as they search the ruins for snipers.
III-SC-200778

Although the 26th *Yankee* Division was on the defensive throughout February, German counterattacks continued to threaten its bridgehead on the east bank of the Saar River. These four photographs, taken in Saarlautern, illustrate the dangers encountered clearing the towns and villages along the Siegfried Line. Mortar fire forces two GIs to hide in doorways while a machinegun crew set up their weapon.   111-SC200704

Go! Go! Go! While the machinegun team gives covering fire, the rest of the squad run forward knowing that snipers could be waiting to take aim from every doorway and window. The process had to be repeated house-by-house, street-by-street, against a determined and resourceful enemy fighting for their homeland.
111-SC200706

Sniper! Mortar and artillery fire bring buildings crashing to the ground while snipers, roaming amongst the rubble, turned street fighting into a deadly game of cat and mouse. A fleeting glimpse of a figure in the ruins and this GI fires off a shot in the hope of silencing an observation post. 111-SC200705

All Clear! Having cleared one street the machinegun crew runs forward weighed down by their weapons and ammunition to join the rest of the squad.
111-SC-200782

While the Allied main offensives were underway in the north, Seventh Army concentrated on reducing the Colmar Pocket, a large salient in the centre of its sector. These infantry of the French First Army hug the walls of a building in Colmar as a Sherman tank blasts an enemy strongpoint.
111-SC-199957

By 3 February Seventh US Army and the First French Army had cleared Colmar and the local population turned out to welcome their mayor as he returned to office after four years in exile. German resistance crumbled once the town had fallen and by the middle of the month 6th Army Group had erased the pocket. 111-SC-199977

With Colmar city cleared, General Patch could turn his attentions to reducing the rest of the Pocket and began his attacks on 17 February. Engineers of 275th Combat Engineers Battalion man a reserve position behind 70th Division's line south of Saarbrucken in case German troops try to break out of the Pocket. 111-SC-200034

Snipers often stayed behind once the main body of troops had withdrawn to prepared positions. This patrol of the 35th *Lone Star* Division crouches and looks for snipers as they reconnoitre a ruined village on the road to Unterbruch as the Germans withdrew from the Colmar Pocket towards the Rhine.
111-SC-200086

Tank destroyers of 636th Tank destroyer Battalion advance in support of 36th *Texas* Division's attack through the war torn streets of Rohrwiller.
111-SC-200031

The enemy can **SHELL** you!

DON'T BUNCH

Technician George Tokum pauses to read a sign warning of the dangers of enemy artillery fire as
35th Division moves through Heinberg during Seventh Army's drive towards the Siegfried Line.
111-SC-200085

These two soldiers of the 70th *Trailblazers* Division take timeout and study the latest pin-up during a lull in the fighting around Spicheren. The division had just captured the high ground overlooking Saarbrucken at the start of Seventh Army's advance towards the Saar River.   111-SC-201063

An M-8 Gun carriage of the 106th Cavalry Group fires its' 76mm Howitzer during 3rd Division's attack on Geislautern in southwest Germany. The Allies were backed up by an impressive logistics chain that kept the front line troops well supplied with ammunition as this pile of empty shell-cases illustrates. 111-SC-200259

The motto of 44th Division, 'Prepared in all things' has stood this patrol in good stead as it advances through the woods around Woefling during Seventh Army's push to the Siegfried Line. Having killed one German sniper two GIs advance cautiously while a third keeps watch.
111-SC-200748

Right: Street fighting was dangerous and close cooperation between the tanks and infantry was essential. This radioman takes instructions from his platoon commander as he directs a Sherman tank towards an enemy outpost.
111-SC-200653

In the woods east of Sarreguemines in Seventh Army's area this group of GIs have done their best to make themselves comfortable. Sergeant John Bronzina repeats new orders for Sergeant Philip Brewer to write down; in the background Private Harold Kelly makes the coffee while Technician Carl Long studies 44th Division's magazine, GI Comics. Many divisions printed a regular bulletin filled with news, jokes and comic strips. 111-SC-201065

A Sherman tank of the 25th Tank Battalion rolls along a ruined street as 14th Liberator Armoured Division supports 35th Infantry Division's attack on Oberhoffen. The tank commander peers carefully from his turret in case snipers lie in wait in the rubble. 111-SC-200654

As the front line pushed forward towards Germany, thousands of civilians were forced to leave their homes and escape the fighting. These French refugees have gathered together all they can carry in their hand cart and are making their way through the streets of Obberhoffen. 111-SC-200032

The Germans abandoned tons of munitions and equipment as they fell back behind the Siegfried Line. These French children, who have grown up knowing nothing but occupation and war, play with an abandoned cache of weapons, blissfully unaware of the dangers. 111-SC-200649

Sniping was a specialist art and this coach is training these men of the 45th *Thunderbird* Division at Seventh Army's sniper school.   111-SC-280422

A British soldier takes on German snipers holding out in ruined factory buildings across the Rhine river near Emmerich.

Chapter Two

The Drive to the Rhine

OPERATION GRENADE opened on 23 February taking the Germans by surprise and by nightfall Ninth Army was firmly established on the far bank of the great barrier formed by the River Roer. Simpson unleashed his armour four days later and the tanks advanced quickly towards Dusseldorf in the east and Wesel in the north. Link up with the Canadians was finally made on 5 March and, despite the delays, over 36,000 Germans were killed or captured before they could withdraw across the river. Unfortunately, the Rhine still remained a barrier. Each time Allied troops drew close, German engineers sent bridges crashing into the river. Field Marshal Montgomery would have to make an assault crossing to the north of the Ruhr.

With 21 Army Group firmly established along the Rhine, it was 12 Army Group's turn to drive to the river and on 1 March General Bradley launched Operation Lumberjack. Again the plan was to conduct a two front pincer movement, First Army in the north and Third Army in the south, in the hope of trapping thousands of Germans before they could escape to the east bank.

First Army made rapid progress over the Erft River and headed southeast towards the confluence of the Ahr and Rhine Rivers. By 5 March the Rhine was in sight at Cologne. As Hodges' troops turned south, driving along the west bank of the river to link up with Third Army's advance northeast towards Koblenz, luck played its part. on 7 March at the small riverside town of Remagen.

A spotter plane had noticed that the Ludendorff rail bridge was still standing and as a task force of the 9th Armoured Division moved through the town of Remagen demolitions rocked the structure. To everyone's surprise the bridge was still standing and as Lieutenant Timmermann's Gls ran across the damaged structure the news shocked both the Allied and German High Commands. By chance, rather than design, the Allies had a captured a bridge over the Rhine.

In the days that followed the Germans tried to destroy the bridge, employing saboteurs, the Luftwaffe, artillery and even V2 rockets, but to no avail and by the time the bridge finally collapsed on 17 March Bradley had five divisions on the east bank. Despite the opportunities offered, Eisenhower stuck to his original plan and ordered First Army to hold a ten-mile deep bridgehead in the hope of drawing German reserves from Montgomery's front to the north.

Meanwhile, 6 Army Group launched Operation UNDERTONE on 15 March as Seventh Army attacked the important Saar area. 12 Army Group's success meant that Third Army could cooperate and with a new revised plan to hand, General Patton turned south into General Patch's sector allowing Seventh Army to concentrate on breaking the Siegfried Line. Third Army advanced quickly toward Oppenheim and Kaiserslautern on the Rhine and once Seventh Army had broken free from the pillboxes and minefields across its' front General Patch had cleared the Saar-Palatinate triangle.

The two Armies met on 20 March, having crushed the German Seventh Army. The pincer movement had also forced the German First Army into a hopeless salient; it was only a matter of time before the entire west bank of the Rhine was in Allied hands.

Eisenhower's plan for the advance into Germany.

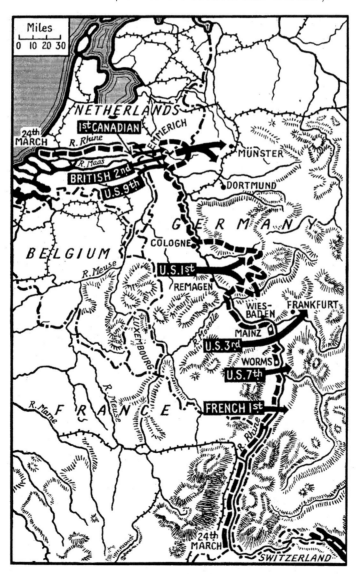

Operation Grenade is underway. Each man carried enough ammunition and rations to last three days and these GIs prepare their packs and check weapons before moving out. The Germans will be amassing reserves on the far bank ready to counterattack and it could be several days before fresh supplies reach the frontline.

The initial assault has been successful and it was essential to keep pushing troops across in accordance with a strict timetable. This group of soldiers wait for the order to move out prepared foxholes near the riverbank.

At the allotted hour each squad grabs an assault boat and begins the final, dangerous, approach to the river. Note that each man has an inflatable life preserver tied around his waist in case his boat capsizes.

The riverbank is in sight but the German artillery has the crossing point well covered. A salvo of shells has forced this squad to hit the dirt as they wait for the signal to cross.

Standing waist deep in the freezing water, two men steady the boat while a squad crams into an assault boat; an operation that had to be practised many times.

Two men paddle furiously while a third steers a course across the fast flowing river. Germans had blown the sluices on the Schwammenauel Dam before American troops could stop them, delaying Ninth Army's attack for several days. By 23 February the floods had subsided but the Roer was still a fast flowing torrent.

Abandoned assault boats and a stricken amphibious vehicle litter the cratered riverbank after the troops have left.

As the floodwaters subsided from the Roer valley, leaving a sea of stinking mud, Ninth Army could begin to advance towards the Rhine. Soaked to the skin and covered in mud, these GIs make their way carefully across a narrow footbridge into the expanding bridgehead.

Canadian infantry and armour moving up to attack the German town of Calcar. German civilians experience the disruption of war as it becomes their turn to know the misery of becoming a refugee.

By the spring of 1945 the Allies had overwhelming numbers of tanks available, however, they were still vulnerable to German anti-tank weapons such as the feared 88s. The crews of 747th Tank Battalion did everything to improve their chances of survival as they prepared to support 29th Division's attack across the Roer River. After welding tank treads and stacking sandbags on the front of their machines mesh and camouflage netting was added. I I I-SC-207289

With the Siegfried Line in tatters, Von Rundstedt's Armies fell back behind the Rhine to regroup while German engineers destroyed the river bridges in their wake.

All along the river rearguards held onto the bridges for as long as they could to allow as many men as possible to escape. The 104th *Timberwolves* Division ran into heavy fighting as it drew close to the bridges in the city of Cologne; all of them were destroyed.

After crossing the Roer River, First Army began its drive to the Rhine looking to cut off large numbers of German troops on the west bank. New tanks like this Pershing, armed with a 90mm gun, joined the armoured divisions in the hope of evening up the balance of power against the heavier German tanks. 111-SC-455227

With the Allies ruling the skies, Eisenhower's armour was able to roam free as it drove to the Rhine. 9th Armoured Division spearheaded First Army's drive towards the sector between Cologne and Coblenz.

However, once again heavy rain and thick mud threatened to slow the Allied advance to a crawl, allowing many Germans to escape across the Rhine. These GIs have hitched a ride as they move closer to the river.
111-SC-202207

Rearguards did what they could to stall First Army in the hope of allowing their comrades to escape behind Germany's final barrier. This tank pushes past a roadblock as villagers display a white flag to show that the soldiers have left.

111-SC-203183

Field Marshal von Rundstedt's plan was to draw his Armies back across the Rhine and regroup behind the river, blowing up the bridges before the Allies could take them. The plan was working until 7 March when the explosives placed on the Ludendorff Bridge at Remagen failed to work. Although the bridge was severely damaged, armoured infantry of the 9th Armoured Division crossed under heavy fire and established a foothold on the east bank. 111-SC-202786

Troops 'cross the Rhine with dry feet, courtesy of the 9th Armoured Division'. For several days First Army's link with the east bank was limited to a single-track road across the bridge. 111-SC-203736

Dodging and weaving as they ran, infantry crossed the Ludendorff Bridge on the afternoon of 7 March while machine guns on the far bank tried to keep them at bay. Once taken, engineers worked around the clock to repair the damaged bridge while German artillery and planes tried in vain to bring the structure down.
111-SC-202370

As the news spread, reinforcements begin heading towards Remagen creating huge traffic jams around the town. Tanks, halftracks and infantry had to wait their turn before filing onto the east bank.
111-SC-202358

Rafts, landing craft and amphibious vehicles ferried men and equipment across the river to help stem the German counterattacks.
111-SC-222569

Within days some of the longest temporary bridges built during the war were in operation; Germany's final barrier had been breached.

291st Engineer Combat Battalion completed the first bridge in less than seventy-two hours despite several direct hits from German artillery fire. Military police had to work around the clock to keep the traffic moving. 111-SC-411818

Infantry of the 9th Division were some of the first to arrive in Remagen and ready to live up to their nickname, *Hitler's Nemesis*. This column of men was pictured marching down the main street towards the bridge; they faced hard fighting in the wooded hills of the Westerwald on the east bank. 111-SC-201876

Day after day Luftwaffe pilots circled above the river, looking to destroy the bridges. The American's responded by deploying the heaviest concentration of anti-aircraft weapons ever gathered during the war. The German's also fired a number of V-2 rockets, experimental terror weapons, at the bridge in an attempt to bring it down. 111-SC-380371

The engineer's attempts to repair the Ludendorff Bridge were ultimately in vain. The combination of enemy fire and heavy traffic, added to the original damage, finally took their toll and the structure toppled over on 17 March. Temporary bridges were able to keep the troops on the east bank supplied and the fledgling bridgehead would continue to draw in German reserves from other parts of the front.

111-SC-202823

Saboteurs armed with explosives tried swimming down the Rhine in the hope of destroying First Army's bridges; they were spotted with powerful searchlights and taken prisoner.
111-SC-207478

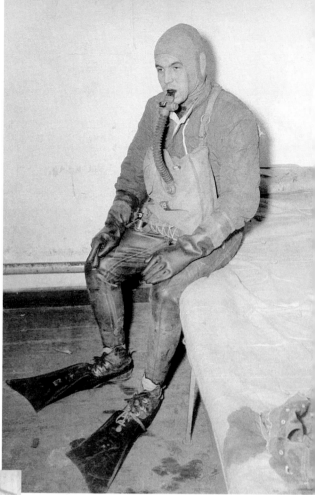

As the Germans reeled from the shock of the capture of the bridge at Remagen, fighting continued all along the river but one by one the Allied Armies drew up alongside the west bank. This GI of the 65th *Battleaxe* Division has just killed one sniper in the ruins of Fraulautern and is on the look out for more.
111-SC-202975

Chapter Three

Crossing the Rhine

BY 22 MARCH all three of the Allied Army Groups had reached the Rhine and in First Army's sector a small bridgehead east of Remagen had drawn German reserves to the area. Now was the time for Eisenhower to unleash 21 Army Group, poised along the river between Rees and Rheinberg northwest of the Ruhr. However, before Montgomery could strike General Patton stole the limelight on the night of 22 March. 5th Division slipped units across the Rhine ten miles south of Mainz, surprising the German troops on the far bank, and by the end of day had established a five-mile deep bridgehead. Hours before Montgomery's attack began Bradley announced to the press that he was across the Rhine without the help of air strikes or airborne troops, a dig at Montgomery's painstaking preparations.

For two weeks troops and equipment had been pouring into 21 Army Group's area while the Allied air forces targeted roads and railways across northern Germany. Over 11,000 sorties were flown during the final hours, culminating in a crushing bombardment of the German positions on the east bank of the river.

Operation Varsity began at 21:00 hours on 23 March and over the next six hours Second British Army and Ninth US Army crossed at five places across a twenty-mile front. The following morning hundreds of planes and gliders flew overhead dropping two airborne divisions just beyond the expanding bridgehead, seizing bridges across the Lippe Canal around Hamminkeln and by nightfall had linked up with the ground troops. The meticulously planned operation had succeeded in breaching the Rhine barrier, opening a way into northern Germany.

Although German counterattacks stalled the Allied advance north and east of Wesel, the delay was only temporary and on 28 March a breakthrough was made and paratroopers of the US 17th Airborne Division raced twenty-five miles to Halten mounted on British tanks. General Simpson had soon pushed his armour through the gap and advanced another forty miles over the next two days, cutting the road and rail routes into the Ruhr; phase one of the Allied plan had been accomplished.

As 21 Army Group battled its' way forward, Eisenhower gave Bradley the order to break out of the Remagen bridgehead and on 25 March First Army attacked. By the end of the first day Hodges' had broken the crust of German defences and his armour passed through, pushing east to the Lahn River before turning north to meet Ninth Army. Third Army made further assault crossings of the Rhine north and south of Mainz, covering 12 Army Group's southern flank as it drove deep into German territory. The advance was rapid but near Paderborn fanatical troops supported by sixty tanks made a determined stand around an SS Panzer training centre. The stronghold was quickly taken with help from General Simpson's troops moving down from the north and by 1 April Ninth and First Army had encircled the Ruhr trapping Field Marshal Model's Army Group B in the pocket.

With German resistance crumbling and all three Army Group's across the Rhine, it was time to unleash the final part of Eisenhower's plan; a series of deep drives into Germany.

Engineers had bridges across the river within twenty-four hours of the assault crossing. 17th Armoured Engineer Battalion built this example for the 2nd Armoured Division, as it joined Ninth Army's drive to encircle the Ruhr. Before long the tanks and halftracks would be racing across northern Germany, living up to the division's nickname – *Hell on Wheels*.

As soon as it as light, rafts and landing craft were ferrying tanks onto the east bank of the Rhine. These two motorboats are helping to steer this raft and its M10 tank destroyer to the far shore. 111-SC-203291

The Wesel road out of Geldern is crowded with British armour and vehicles as Second Army prepares to drive into northern Germany.

At first light on 24 March two Airborne Division's, the 6th British and 17th American, mustered on aerodromes across England and France ready to make the last major combat jump of the war.

Men and equipment are packed tightly inside a glider ready for take off. Axes and hammers are close at hand in case the doors jam as the glider crashes on the landing zone.
111-SC-203298

Hundreds of transport planes and gliders climb into the sky over Paris as the vast air armada begins to gather.

After braving the curtain of anti-aircraft fire the glider pilots had to pick an area free of fences, hedges, telegraph wires or ditches, to ensure a safe landing. Dozens were shot down or crashed but enough men survived to take on the German positions. After orientating themselves, this group of men will head off towards their assembly point. 111-SC-202655

German anti-aircraft guns opened fire as soon as the first wave of planes crossed over the Rhine. This pilot scans the horizon for landmarks as he prepares to steer his cumbersome glider to the ground. 111-SC-202650

Many paratroopers were dropped far from their drop zone and it was several hours before all the objectives had been taken. This British paratrooper and his American counterpart, who has landed on the wrong drop zone, take cover from enemy fire.

With no time to waste these glider troops unload a trailer full of supplies on the landing zone. The huge mass of the Waco glider was an inviting target for German gun crews.

The 17th Airborne Division lives up to its' nickname, Thunder from Heaven. Despite heavy losses in the first few minutes, combat teams formed quickly and moved in on the German positions. As one paratrooper gets untangled from his parachute; his comrades round up the first batch of prisoners taken on the drop zone.

As the war drew to a close both young and old joined the ranks of the Armed forces to fight the Allies. These frightened members of the Hitler Youth have surrendered to a well-armed paratrooper.

Despite heavy losses during the landing, the paratroopers began to gain the upper hand and by nightfall contact had been made with the British troops crossing the river; 21 Army Group's bridgehead over the Rhine was secure.

XVIII Airborne Corps' casualties had been high, but by nightfall Montgomery had a bridgehead over twenty miles wide and up to five miles deep. Now it was time to unleash Operation Plunder, the drive into northern Germany.

Bruised and bloodied, this young paratrooper takes a moment to reflect on his first combat jump. First aid packs had been strapped to the front of helmets as an unofficial means of identification.

Thick woods on Ninth US Army's front threatened to stall the breakout. 30th Infantry Division, known as the *Old Hickories*, had to clear Staatsforst Wesel before General Simpson could unleash his armoured divisions. 111-SC-270968

After overrunning the German division covering the east bank of the Rhine, these GIs head towards Dorsten on the far side of the woods aided by an M24 Chaffee tank. 111-SC-270973

Contact! Army Group H deployed *116th Panzer Division* against Ninth Army, meeting 30th Division head on in the woods east of the Rhine. After hitching a ride on this tank this squad dismount ready to deploy into the forest.

Anxious moments as shells rain down and bullets ricochet through the trees. Battle groups comprising tanks and halftracks full of panzergrenadiers blocked every road on 30th Division's front. 111-SC-270972

Medic! One man is down, but his buddies have no time to help; German armour is bearing down on their position.

British Shermans on the move towards Geilenkirchen watched by an American infantryman from a ruined building.

The fight is over, but it is only one of many in a three-day battle for Staatsforst Wesel. A German halftrack armed with a 20mm flak gun stands smoking, having fallen foul of the Chaffee's while the weight of American artillery has dispersed the rest of the enemy battle group. III-SC-203439

In Third Army's sector General Patton was preparing his own assault crossings. These trucks are carrying men of the 76th *Onaway* Division over the Moselle River at Hasenport en route for the Rhine.
111-SC-204163

Terrain rather than German resistance poised the problem in Third Army's sector where the Rhine flowed quickly through a high sided gorge. Machine gun fire opens up from the far bank as smoke drifts across the river, forcing the waiting soldiers to hug the ground.

87th Infantry Division, the *Golden Acorns*, made the first crossing at Boppard and as this DUKW, a small amphibious truck, pulls up ready to make the crossing the soldiers waste no time scrambling on board.

With nowhere to hide everyone hugs the floor of the DUKW as the driver struggles to steer his DUKW across the fast flowing river. Although the crossing only took a few minutes it would have seemed like a lifetime.

As soon as the heights on the far bank had been taken, Navy units could bring their landing craft down to the riverbank, speeding up the flow of men and materials across the river. It is smiles all round for this platoon.

Before long the engineers had built their treadway bridges across the Boppard gorge allowing armour to move across and secure the crossing. These tanks of the 735th Tank Battalion would soon be joining the infantry on the heights.

GIs of the 89th Division, the *'Rolling W'*, paddle furiously to reach the far side of the river at St Goar.
111-SC-204166

These men hug the bottom of their DUKW as it makes the terrifying journey across the river.

Having survived the crossing there is no time to waste. These GIs are eager to get off the exposed river bank and head into the town.

By the end of March all of Eisenhower's Armies had bridgeheads on the far bank. Seventh Army established a bridgehead at Worms to cover General Patton's flank. 85th Engineer Battalion named this bridge after their General.
111-SC-207858

General Patch also used the Mannheim crossing in Third Army's sector to ferry troops across the river.
111-SC-205841

With thousands of Allied troops pouring across the Rhine, the stage was set for a rapid advance deep into Germany. 7th Armoured Division led First Army's breakout of the Remagen bridgehead; these GIs are fighting a running battle with snipers in the town of Melhem.

Old men and young boys joined the fight for the Fatherland. Soldiers of the 94th Division, nicknamed the *Neuf-Cats,* captured these two teenagers in Frankenthal.

111-SC-204183

Following a tour of the east bank of the Rhine, General Eisenhower announced to the world on 27 March that, '*the Germans as a military force on the western front are a whipped army.*' The beginning of the end was in sight.
111-SC-204193

Chapter Four

The drive across Germany

BY THE BEGINNING OF APRIL every one of the Allied Armies had a bridgehead on the east bank of the Rhine and had started to drive deep into Germany. With their last barrier breached, and a large part of their Army encircled in the Ruhr pocket, the situation was looking grim for the Wehrmacht. Day after day armoured columns made great advances, making use of Hitler's autobahns to drive east, carving through the German Armies with ease.

On 28 March Eisenhower announced his new plan to keep pace with the rapidly changing situation. After clearing the Ruhr, Bradley's Army group would head the advance looking to meet Russian troops as quickly as possible and cut the German forces in two. Meanwhile, 21 Army Group would head northeast towards the Baltic coast to isolate enemy troops stationed in Denmark. On the south flank General Devers had to drive deep into Bavaria and Austria to prevent fanatical troops gathering in the mountains and forming the rumoured 'National Redoubt'.

Ninth and First Army began to attack the Ruhr on 4 April and before long German resistance collapsed, leaving 325,000 prisoners in Allied hands; thousands of prisoners of war and slave labourers were also freed. On Third Army's front troops found vast quantities of gold bars, paper currency and art treasures in a salt mine, all hidden away by the Nazis. Close by another grim discovery was made at the small town of Ohrdruf, it was the first of many concentration camps. For the first time the real inhumanity of the Nazi's Final Solution could be seen at first hand.

Meanwhile, the Allied pursuit continued relentlessly and by 9 April both First and Ninth Armies had crossed the Leine River and were heading towards the Elbe. General Simpson was anxious to reach Berlin before the Russians and his armoured spearheads reached the river, only 50 miles short of the capital, by the 11th. However, Eisenhower wanted to concentrate on destroying the German military and agreed to use the Elbe and Mulde Rivers as boundaries.

All across Germany resistance was collapsing as the Allies roamed freely, finding white flags decorating many towns and villages. While pockets of resistance were rapidly crushed. One group of 70,000 determined soldiers held out for several days in the Harz Mountains, but the majority of German troops lay down their arms after a token show of resistance.

On 6th Army's Group's front Seventh Army took several days to break out of its bridgehead, south of Frankfurt, but German resistance melted away as soon as

General Patch's armour broke free. Fierce battles in towns such as Aschaffenburg and Heilbronn did little to stem the advance and by 15 April both Seventh and Third Army were turning south towards Austria. Thousands of German soldiers surrendered and white flags hung from every window as General Devers' men drove down the Danube valley; it was clear that all but a few hardened Nazis believed the war was over. The final bastion en route to the National Redoubt, Nuremberg, was taken on 20 April and Stuttgart fell the following day to the First French Army.

The Ruhr was a metropolis of domestic and industrial buildings, many laid waste by the Allied bombing campaign. While Ninth Army pushed into the ruins, First Army attacked the woods to the south. This GI warily makes his way through the rubble on the look out for snipers.

Amongst the rubble and debris of the towns across the Ruhr, individual battles were fought as infantry squads, machinegun and mortar crews contested every block and every house. Another suspected stronghold receives a burst of machine gun fire.

Clearing the ruins was nerve-racking and dangerous. These two men have just spotted signs of movement as their platoon moves cautiously forward through a bomb-damaged factory.

Tanks and infantry had to work in close cooperation during the battle. The infantry needed the tanks to take out bunkers and strongpoints; the tanks needed the infantry to keep panzerfaust teams at bay. This Sherman has been fitted with a bulldozer blade to help carve a route through the rubble.

Inching forward, First Army worked its way through the towns and forests of the Ruhr to squeeze Fifteenth Army into the Pocket. This machine gun crew have a road intersection covered in case the rest of their company flush any German troops out of the ruins.
111-SC-204149

A sharp eye and nerves of steel were needed during street fighting. A shot rings out in a narrow street and this GI is faced with a dilemma. Which window is the sniper hiding behind or, as was often the case, has he withdrawn to a new position? This man is hoping that a burst of automatic fire will decide the issue, allowing his advance to continue.
111-SC-341780

After making an assault crossing of the Sieg River during First Army's attack on the Ruhr Pocket, 97th *Trident* Division encountered light resistance in the town of Siegburg. These GIs are moving warily down a street on the look out for snipers and machine gun posts.
111-SC-341771

A poor road network hampered First Army's advance to begin with but German resistance melted away in the face of coordinated attacks. These GIs are keeping a lookout for signs of movement as they await orders to move into Saalhausen.
111-SC-205946

97th Division followed up the German withdrawal and after heavy fighting captured Düsseldorff. A sniper has pinned down this squad behind a ruined church; the GIs scan the surrounding buildings for signs of life before returning fire.
111-SC-341773

Organised resistance collapsed after the fall of Düsseldorff, however, some fanatics preferred to fight on. A machine has pinned this squad down behind a low wall and the GIs shout instructions to each other as they try to locate the weapon.
111-SC-341779

Time for a change of ownership. Neither leader would live to the end of the war; President Theodore Roosevelt died of natural causes on 12 April; Hitler committed suicide as the month came to an end.

The Ruhr Pocket finally capitulated on 18 April leaving the Allies with a new problem to solve; 325,000 prisoners had to be guarded and processed. Many were held in temporary camps, comprising nothing more than an open field surrounded by barbed wire fences. This group is a small part of the 82,000 prisoners taken by XVIII Airborne Corps and held at Gummersbach. 111-SC-204318

Lieutenant Byron Hansford, a military policeman of the 99th *Battle Babes* Division, questions three senior German officers taken in the Ruhr Pocket. Four months earlier the division had been fighting for its life, trying to contain the German offensive in the Ardennes. How fortunes have changed.
111-SC-205846

While thousands of Germans marched into captivity a few preferred to fight to the death, sniping at US troops from the ruins. This squad of 95th *Victory* Division have just come under sniper fire in the Mundelheim district of Dortmund and a house displaying a white flag has come under suspicion.
111-SC-206225

After eliminating the Ruhr Pocket, Ninth Army turned east in the hope of reaching Berlin before the Russians. After crossing the Leine River the 83rd *Thunderbolt* Division helped to scatter the German stronghold in the Harz Mountains, reaching the Elbe on 13 April. These men are keeping up the rapid pace of the advance as they march through Langelsheim.
111-SC-34178

This group of German prisoners are probably cursing their comrades' efficiency as they shelter from artillery fire behind the tank destroyer, *Cynthia Queen*.

During the early months of the year thick mud restricted movement off the road but as soon as the weather improved in April, the Allies were able to deploy their superior numbers of tanks and half-tracks anywhere. This group of Shermans are firing indirectly in support of an infantry attack.

As the months passed Allied tank design improved, in an attempt to match the larger and heavier German models. Even so crews were allowed to use their own initiative to improve their machines by gathering useful equipment and making field modifications. The original profile of this tank destroyer is lost under a pile of sandbags, spares and personal equipment; the forked prongs were useful for carving a way through embankments and hedges.

Carefully concealed anti-tank guns could stop an armoured attack in its tracks but close cooperation between the tanks crews, the armoured infantry and the self-propelled artillery usually had an answer for all tactical situations. The crew of this Sherman, nicknamed the Ronson because of its tendency to burst into flames when hit, has paid the ultimate price for getting caught in the open.

1st Division, the 'Big Red One', crossed the Weser River on 8 April as it spearheaded First Army's advance towards the Elbe River. Artillery fire pounds the wooded hills overlooking the river while the infantry paddle furiously to the far bank.
111-SC-207392

First Army encountered sporadic resistance during the drive to the Elbe. This machine gun team are running forward to a new firing position to assist a platoon pinned down by enemy fire.

Covering fire! While the team pour a stream of bullets towards the enemy occupied building, their buddies withdraw to safety, ready to regroup and attack once more.

The Sherman Calliope, a tank mounted launcher armed with sixty rockets, was the Allied response to the German Nebelwerfer, a fearsome weapon known by the troops as the *Screaming Meemie*; a reference to the terrifying noise the rockets made as they hurtled towards their target.

British infantry move into a village that has just been captured in a joint attack by American and British troops.

Another German town has been laid waste by heavy street fighting. Tired and weary after their exertions, this platoon has hitched a lift on a passing tank as it pushes on to the next objective.

This SS soldier stood little chance against 748th Tank Battalion's Shermans as they supported 89th Division attack on Blankenheim. The division lived up to its nickname, the *Rolling W*, as it swept through Thuringia towards the Mulde River. 111-SC-206228

Having reached the River Elbe on 12 April, 5th Armoured Division was only forty-five miles from Berlin and well on the way to living up to its' nickname – the *Victory Division*. However, Eisenhower recalled his troops from the east bank of the river to await the Russians. 5th Armoured was ordered to turn west to destroy the *Von Clausewitz Panzer Division* at Klotze. The local population stand in silence as this column of tanks passes through their town. 111-SC205881

The first meeting between Allied and Soviet troops took place near Leckwitz on 25 April on the River Mulde. The following day these three soldiers, one British, one American and one Russian, shared a pack of cigarettes a short distance away at Torgau. 111-SC-205353

Private John Lyons and Technician Alfred Weiland greet Major Nikolai Harlanhoff on the outskirts of Apollensdorf in Ninth Army's sector.
111-SC-207823

Put it there! Lieutenant-General Courtney Hodges greets Major-General Backenov, XXXIV Corps commander, at Torgau on the banks of the River Elbe.
111-SC-204953

Seventh Army encountered heavy resistance during the early stages of its advance and 45th *Thunderbird* Division had to fight for every house and street in the ruins of Aschaffenburg.   111-SC-204184

Built up areas were dangerous places for tanks. Snipers and panzerfaust teams could move freely through the ruins and fire from close range before slipping away to a new hiding place. Tanks of 191st Tank Battalion make use of this park to engage snipers from a safe distance during the attack on Aschaffenburg. 111-SC-204185

The Allied tank crews did not always have it their own way. A Panzerfaust team disabled these two Shermans during 14th Armoured Division's attack on Lohr. After the first tank was hit, the driver of the second machine reversed into a building as he tried to escape to safety. 111-SC-206838

GIs of the 19th Armoured Infantry Battalion run through the smoking ruins of Hoolrich as 14th Armoured Division advances towards the Danube.
111-SC-206836

11th Armoured Division lived up to its' nickname as it raced like a *Thunderbolt* during Third Army's drive down the Danube valley. The crew of this tank were taking no chances as they moved through Kronach, firing a number of shells into a potential strongpoint.
111-SC-206223

German rearguards tried to stall the American advance with roadblocks but a lack of heavy weapons and artillery support usually meant that their efforts were in vain. This Sherman of 191st Tank Battalion gives covering fire with its' .03 machine guns during 45th Division's battle for Bamberg.
111-SC-206230

71st *Red Circle* Division cleared Coburg on 13 April and cut the autobahn connecting Munich and Berlin, the main route south for German troops heading for the National Redoubt. Although white flags decorate the walls, this squad has had to call up a tank of 761st Tank Battalion after coming under sniper fire. 111-SC-207693

Having killed one German soldier, this squad wade across the Schleuse stream. 26th *Yankee* Division took part in Third Army's advance into Austria, attacking Waldau en route where it found the main German force holding the surrounding pine forests. 111-SC-341768

The GIs hit the dirt as mortar and small arms opens fire from a hedge line beyond the watercourse.

Return Fire! As the squad leader looks for targets his men give covering fire in the hope of driving the German rearguard away.

The Allies had to cross watercourses of every shape and size creating a huge logistical headache for the engineers. Bridges had to erected at top speed to keep the advance moving and sometimes mistakes were made. This Sherman of 714th Tank Battalion has just broken through a wooden trestle bridge during 12th Armoured Division's advance. Although this tank drove its' way out of trouble, the rest of the column would have to wait until a small treadway bridge had been installed
111-SC-208021

12th Armoured Division lived up to their nickname, the *Hellcats,* during their rapid drive to the Danube, capturing the bridge at Dillingen before the German engineers could destroy it. The bridge allowed Seventh Army to flood into southern Germany towards the National Redoubt. These men of Combat Command B would have no doubt translated the village name Krautsosheim into *'Home of the Krauts'*.
111-SC-263520

Sergeant Willis Cochrun is taking no chances during 4th Division's battle for Rothenburg, part of Seventh Army's drive into Bavaria. Apart from his rifle, Cochrun has extra pistols, knives and bags of grenades strapped to his body. 111-SC-206447

A captured German NCO of the *Fallschirmjäger* (paratrooper), having escaped from a burning house, is escorted by a British officer to the ever-growing PoW enclosures.

Third Army's armour became unstoppable as it turned south towards Austria. This M8 Greyhound armoured car and Sherman tank are shelling German positions on the outskirts of Kessler before moving into the village.
111-SC-206350

White flags greet this halftrack of 10th Armoured Division as it enters Geiselhardt. The *Tigers* spearheaded Seventh Army's drive to the Danube, reaching the river on 23 April.
111-SC-205871

One of the triumphs of Hitler's regime was the autobahn system criss-crossing the Reich but in the spring of 1945 Allied armoured divisions made use of the motorways to speed across Germany. These men of 63rd Division have hitched a ride on one of 12th Armoured Division's tanks during Seventh Army's drive towards the National Redoubt. 111-SC-206022

116th Reconnaissance Squadron leads 12th Armoured Division through Weilheim during Seventh Army's drive through Bavaria. The lightly armed reconnaissance vehicles scouted ahead of the tanks looking to bypass centres of resistance.
111-SC-207626

Seventh Army captured 24,000 prisoners during the drive to the Danube and had to establish a prisoner of war camp in Worms. Regular soldiers, Volksstrum conscripts in their sixties and teenage Hitler Youth volunteers mingle with Regular Army troops in the cities main square.
111-SC-205842

This thirteen-year old boy was one of a group of sixty Hitler Youth members captured in Martinszell by 14th Armoured Division. The boys, with ages ranging from seventeen to thirteen, had been expected to keep the American advance at bay with machine pistols and bazookas. 111-SC-207470

As 6th Army Group broke through the German lines and raced towards the Danube, several high-ranking officers were discovered amongst the thousands of prisoners. Third Army captured Field Marshal von Kleist and Brigadier-General Russwurm, inspector of German Army signal troops, near Mittenfels on 27 April 111-SC-207696

By April the Luftwaffe was finished and even jet fighters, such as this Me262, could not save the Reich from destruction. This fighter squadron began to use a local autobahn as a makeshift landing strip after Allied planes destroyed their airfield. The 63rd *Blood and Fire Division* discovered this example hidden in the woods. 111-SC-206021

This mock up of a fighter plane was found on a dummy aerodrome near the Mulde River in an attempt to draw Allied bombers away from the real target, an airfield near Ohrdue.
111-SC-206349

The Danube barred Seventh Army's route into Bavaria, fortunately German resistance in the area was negligible and in a matter of hours XV Corps had troops on the far bank. These GIs of 45th Division are carrying their assault boat through the undergrowth ready to cross the river.
111-SC-206014

The greatest difficulty faced by these men was getting into the boats without turning them over. Paddling hard while the oarsman steers his boat against the current, these GIs head for the far bank. Many boats were dragged downstream, but by nightfall 45th Division was in a position to resume its advance on Munich.
111-SC-206015

762nd Field Artillery Regiment supported 99th Division's crossing with its' 150mm Howitzers. Once the infantry had established a bridgehead on the far bank 14th Armoured Division drove quickly across the Isar River and lived up to its nickname, the *Liberator Division*, at Moosburg, freeing 110,000 Allied prisoners of war. 111-SC-206003

Tanks of the 20th Armoured Division wait under cover of smoke screen while 42nd Engineer Combat Battalion completes a treadway bridge across the Danube. The division crossed the river on 28 April and drove towards Munich. 111-SC-206011

A mounted anti-aircraft gun of 546th Anti-Aircraft Regiment keeps guard over 65th Division's crossing point as rafts take vehicles across.
111-SC-206040

Lorries belonging to Third Army Combat Engineers carry pontoons down to the Danube where 65th Division crossed at Kapfelberg. Although the German engineers were adept at destroying bridges before they could be captured, their Allied counterparts were equally skilled at building temporary ones.
111-SC-206043

The Danube, 'just another damn river'. German troops destroyed many bridges before they could be taken, leaving plenty of work for the engineers. 160th Engineer Combat Battalion and 993rd Treadway Bridge Company built this example at Regensburg during Third Army's drive towards Austria.
111-SC-206005

Resistance opposite XXI Corps stiffened as it approached Nuremberg. A patrol of 66th Armoured Infantry Battalion have caught a group of Germans withdrawing towards the city and destroyed their ammunition truck, the survivors have withdrawn leaving their dead behind.
111-SC-206446

Between 1930 and 1938 Hitler reviewed his troops at the annual Nuremberg rallies, the highpoint of the Nazi calendar. On 26 April 1945 GIs of the 80th *Blue Ridge* Division gathered around Fuehrer's podium to listen to the *Yankee Doodlers* band. Hitler committed suicide four days later.
111-SC-206058

3rd Division came under machinegun, mortar and sniper fire as it moved into the suburbs of Nuremberg. These GIs are taking cover while a Sherman of 756th Tank Battalion takes on a German position. The city finally fell on 20 April after a three-day battle. 111-SC-206449

Hitler's first step on the road to power began in Munich in 1923 when his supporters tried to seize power. These tanks are waiting for the signal to follow 45th Division's advance into the heart of the city. 111-SC-207740

20th Armoured Division quickly crushed a group of fanatical soldiers at the SS barracks and Antitank School and moved into the city. Civilians wave white handkerchiefs as they watch the American tanks roll by. 111-SC-206195

42nd *Rainbow* Division discovered one of the largest concentration camps at Dachau on the outskirts of Munich. These inmates are healthy enough to greet their liberators as they mingle with the crowds. 32,000 prisoners were freed but thousands more had died at the hands of their brutal guards. 111-SC-206196

One of the huge burial pits discovered by British troops at Belsen concentration camp. Eisenhower saw to it that many of his soldiers entered the camps so they could see the horrors for themselves; thousands of German civilians were also forced to visit. The Holocaust would never be forgotten. 111-SC-204385

Corporal Harry Mutinski has come a long way and seen many sights since he left Philadelphia but none as shocking as the Dachau concentration camp on the outskirts of Munich. Here he is doing his best to share out a pack of cigarettes to the prisoners. 111-SC-207744

The Allies also discovered large stockpiles of money, gold and art treasures hidden away by the Nazis. General Patton's troops discovered £125million of gold bars and a stash of art treasures in a salt mine just outside the town of Merkers. 111-SC-204516

Chapter Five

The Italian Front

While events were unfolding in Germany, plans were underway to restart the Italian campaign after several months of inactivity. At Hitler's insistence, General Heinrich von Vietinghoff's Army Group C had spent the winter months building three defensive lines in the rugged Italian hills. Although the Germans were outnumbered in vehicles, artillery and aircraft, they were hardened veterans, experienced at defensive fighting.

Fifth US Army's first attack began along the Ligurian coast on 5 April and after several days of savage fighting the town of Massa fell to the 92nd *Buffalo* Division. Four days later Eighth British Army unleashed an assault against the German lines along the Adriatic coast and before long British, New Zealander, Polish and Indian troops were pushing north towards the Argenta gap.

Fifth Army's main offensive, codenamed Operation CRAFTSMAN, began on 14 April and after a massive artillery bombardment US troops began to advance across the Reno River and Pra del Bianco valleys and began to scale the mountains beyond. Heavy fighting raged in the Apennines over the next four days but one by one Monte Pigna, Monte Mantino, Monte Mosca and Monte Pero fell to the Americans. The sight of the Stars and Stripes fluttering on top of Monte Adone on 18 April signified the beginning of the end for the Germans and as Fifth Army pushed past the city of Bologna, General Vietinghoff ordered his men to fall back to the River Po.

A high-speed race followed as the Allies chased the Germans to the river and although thousands managed to escape, over 100,000 Axis troops were captured. The first tanks reached the river on 22 April and spread out along the south bank, cutting off the Axis lines of retreat. Two days later GIs of the 88th *Blue Devils* Division crossed the Po River at two places and found little to stop them; it appeared the Germans were struggling to man their second defensive line.

General Truscott decided to keep up the momentum of his advance with the help of amphibious craft, rubber rafts, wooden boats, and ferries and once on the far side his troops commandeered any vehicle they could find to keep moving. Within two days bridges had been built and Fifth Army erupted from its' bridgehead, advancing forty miles in the first twenty-four hours and split Army Group C in two. The Adige Line, a fortified zone up to two miles deep in the Alpine foothills, would have been a tough nut to crack if the Germans had been able to reach it in sufficient numbers. However, with thousands of his men cut off by the Allied armour and most of his artillery and tanks wrecked or abandoned during the retreat, General Vietinghoff had no option but to surrender. His Army Group had been shattered and as Italian partisans took their revenge on Italy's facist dictator, Benito Mussolini, and his supporters, the cease-fire took effect on 2 May. It brought to a close the Italian campaign.

The Germans had sited their defensive lines to make the most of the hills, ravines and valleys of the Apennines Hills and snow and ice made it an inhospitable place for both friend and foe. These troops are digging into the hard ground to make a shelter from the biting wind.

Men of the Grenadier Guards move up to the British forward positions on the Eighth Army front in the Apennines.

Harsh weather conditions and rugged terrain brought offensive operation's to a halt on the Italian front for several months. Winter clothing helps these soldiers of the 34th *Red Bull* Division fight the cold during a mountain patrol though the hills south of Bologna. 111-SC-200228

The Italian campaign was a multinational affair with American, British, Indian, New Zealand, South African and Brazilian troops working together to break through the Apennines. This South African tank crew has been well supplied as it shells German positions in the Monzuno area.
111-SC-200239

Many of the soldiers of the 10th Mountain Division had been skiers and mountaineer before the war, useful skills in the rugged Italian terrain. This member of 86th Regiment is tying part of a 37mm Pack Gun onto the back of a mule before heading into the mountains; it took two mules to carry one complete gun assembly.
111-SC-262704

A flurry of snow showers the crew of a 155mm Gun belonging to 61st Heavy Regiment as they shell German positions opposite 6th South African Division.
111-SC-191306

Round Away! From beneath their camouflage netting a howitzer crew fires at a German hilltop position from 34th Division's lines.
111-SC-262703

After thick fog delayed Operation CRAFTSMAN for two days, General Mark Clark unleashed Fifth Army's artillery on the German positions on 14 April.

This Battery of 105mm self-propelled howitzers adds their weight of firepower to the Allied bombardment.

The rugged landscape of the Apennines was a natural defensive barrier, improved by the Axis troops over the winter months. This squad has just come under fire from a fortified farmhouse as they descend into a valley.

Bitter hand-to-hand fighting marked the Allied assault on the hillsides and the ravines of the Italian Mountains. These two GIs take cover as a white phosphorous grenade explodes in front of a German strongpoint.

During the first few days of the offensive the Allied armour had to wait until the infantry had opened routes through the mountains. In the meantime, tanks and howitzers acted as mobile artillery platforms.

During four days of hard fighting, Fifth Army cleared mountaintop after mountaintop of the Apennines but the raising of the Stars and Stripes on top of Monte Adone on 18 April marked the beginning of the end. Two days later the Allies began a high-speed pursuit to the Po River. General Mark Clark has just visited Rover Joe observation post to watch the battle; he is accompanied by Major-General Geoffrey Keyes, II Corps commanding officer, and General Alphonse Juin, the French chief of staff.
111-SC-208528

The turning point in the battle for the Apennine hills came on the 20 April as both Fifth US and Eighth British Army began a high-speed drive towards the Po River. These Italian paratroopers are crowded into their C-47 transport planes ready to drop behind enemy lines to rally partisans and disrupt the German withdrawal. 111-SC-208523

Reconnaissance troops prepare to spearhead 91st Division's advance into Vergato on the road to Bologna. Teams of men in fast moving jeeps went ahead of the main force to assess the enemy positions. The tank-dozer in the background is clearing rubble from the streets. 111-SC-208376

American troops entered Bologna on 21 April as they raced towards the Po River. Local partisans rose against the retreating Axis forces but once they had fled the Allies took the wise move of disarming the local population, collecting a large stock of rifles, grenades and machineguns. This soldier of 135th Regiment is trying to persuade a partisan to hand over his rifle. 111-SC-207367

The rapid Allied advance from the Apennine Hills cut off thousands of German troops as they withdrew to the Po River. This soldier of the 6th South African Armoured Division looks across the river surrounded by discarded equipment left behind during the retreat. Before long the South Africans would have a bridgehead on the far bank. 111-SC-263015

Fifth Army reached the River Po close on the heels of the retreating Germans, cutting off many on the south bank. These men of 350th Regiment are closing in on a group of trapped enemy soldiers.

At noon on 24 April 88th Division crossed the Po River at two places, meeting patchy resistance on the far bank. The following day more crossings were made and the decision was taken to use every available craft to get across; the German had to be pushed back before they could dig in.

The crew of a 57mm gun target enemy positions on the far bank, part of the artillery barrage covering 88th Division's crossing at Ostigila. 111-SC-207371

Corporal Gregory Perez, a ranger attached to the 88th *Blue Devils* Division, awaits orders to cross the Po River north of Monterumici. 111-SC-207368

As H-Hour approaches GIs of 351st Infantry regiment wait anxiously to cross beneath a ruined bridge. All eyes are fixed on the far bank as the officers search for signs of enemy activity. 111-SC-207372

A line of assault boats laid out ready behind a flood dike awaits the infantry; their resemblance to coffins would not have gone unnoticed.
111-SC-207373

Support waves crossed in amphibious vehicles known as Alligators. GIs of the 351st Infantry Regiment's 3rd Battalion file down to the water's edge ready to cross the river. 111-SC-207375

The group of GIs wave cheerfully to the cameraman as their Alligator pulls away from the shore and heads across the river. The Germans demolished Ostigila Bridge in the background as they withdrew. 111-SC-207376

88th Division was firmly established on the north bank of the river by the evening of 24 April, and prisoners started to flood in as many German soldiers realised the war would soon be over. 111-SC-207374

After crossing the Po River 'at the run' Fifth Army reached the Adige River on 27 April and had crossed before the Germans could throw up a defensive line. GIs of the 91st *Powder River* Division are making use of this damaged bridge to cross the river near Legnago.
111-SC-208340

Within hours of the assault crossing, 1554th Heavy Pontoon Battalion was hard at work building a bridge at San Benedetto. On 25 April Major-General Willis D Crittenberger, IV Corps commander, visited the site to watch the first vehicle cross.
111-SC-207379

While engineers worked around the clock to build bridges across the Po River at Revere, rafts carried tanks and vehicles to the far shore. Amphibious vehicles known as DUKWs ferried men and supplies across.
111-SC-208315

As 402nd Combat Engineer Battalion put the finishing touches to their treadway bridge, Lieutenant-General Geoffrey Keyes, II US Corps commander, and his aide, Louis Pearce made a symbolic crossing on foot.
111-SC-208318

The crew of a Sherman belonging to 757th Tank Battalion shout instructions to their driver as he steers his machine across the Revere treadway bridge. Only one tank can cross at once and the rest of the battalion await their turn on the far bank.
111-SC-208319

The population of Venice turn out to watch their liberators march through the city in a parade staged to recognise the efforts of the local partisans. These British soldiers of the 56th Division lead the march past through San Marco square. 111-SC-208117

As the Allies raced to beat the Axis to the Adige Po, local partisans took over the task of rounding up fascist supporters hiding in the towns and hills. By 24 April they had cleared Piacenza and this colourful partisan poses proudly for an American cameraman. The graffiti on the wall reads 'Viva il Duce'. Four days after this photograph was taken Mussolini was executed near Lake Como by partisans; his body was taken to Piazzale Loreto in Milan and strung up for all to see.
111-SC-208337

Fifth Army's offensive opened on 14 April and savage fighting followed in the Pra del Bianco and Reno River valleys. This Sherman rolls through a devastated village as Fifth Army advanced to the west of Bologna.

By 21 April the Axis forces were falling back at high speed towards the Po River, abandoning Bologna to Fifth Army. These GIs are passing through Casalecchio on the outskirts of the town. 111-SC-208181

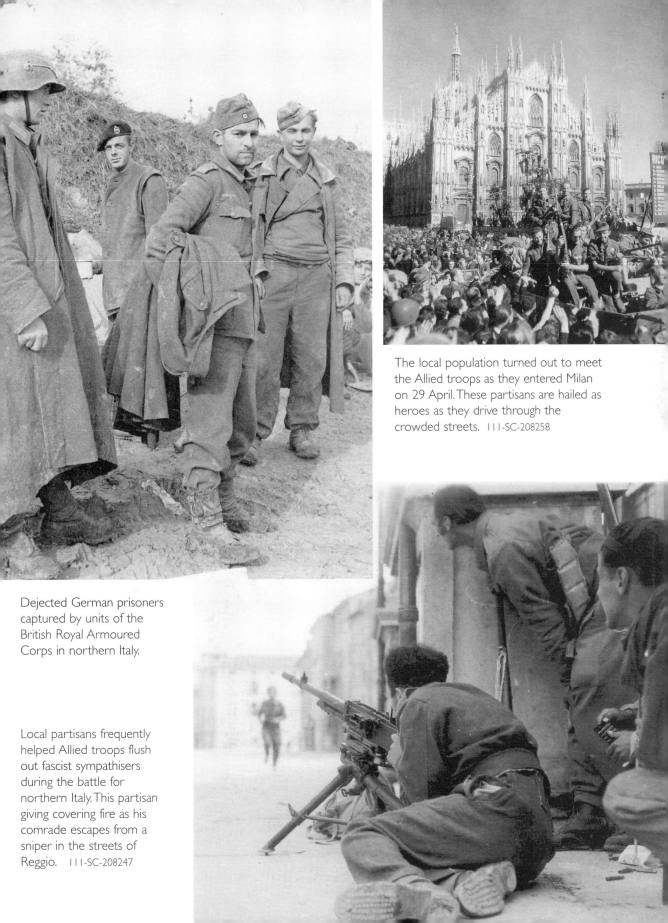

The local population turned out to meet the Allied troops as they entered Milan on 29 April. These partisans are hailed as heroes as they drive through the crowded streets. 111-SC-208258

Dejected German prisoners captured by units of the British Royal Armoured Corps in northern Italy.

Local partisans frequently helped Allied troops flush out fascist sympathisers during the battle for northern Italy. This partisan giving covering fire as his comrade escapes from a sniper in the streets of Reggio. 111-SC-208247

Once the Allies had crossed the Po River, the Axis forces began to fall back to the Adige Line leaving rearguards in the path of 88th Division. One Sherman has been disabled in the street of Vicenza and the crew are carrying their wounded comrade to the aid station. 111-SC-208333

A GI runs across the main square in Vicenza as snipers and mortars try to hold back 88th Division's advance. Burning vehicles, abandoned by the withdrawing Germans, litter the street.
111-SC-208335

Feelings between the partisans and fascist sympathisers ran high after years of living under Mussolini's regime. These partisans have just executed a member of Piacenza's Black shirt militia with a bullet in the back of the head.
111-SC-208336

By the time Fifth Army entered Genoa on 27 April, the 4,000 strong garrison had already surrendered to the local partisans. Two German officers lead a mixed group of soldiers through the city streets as the locals look on; a partisan guards the prisoners. 111-SC-2083349

A Sherman tank drives through Piazza Duoma in Milan as its' commander admires the impressive cathedral, spared from destruction by Army Group C's rapid collapse in the face of the Allies' relentless pursuit across northern Italy. 111-SC-208341

The Pretoria Regiment leads the 6th South African Division through the town of Polona en route to the Adige River while the local population cheers them on. 111-SC-208422

Axis forces had spent months preparing the Adige Line in the Alpine foothills. This bunker, one of many covering Highway 51 in the Cortina di Ampezzo area, was hidden by camouflaged wooden doors. 111-SC-208080

On 4 May in Florence, General Mark Clark handed his instructions for conducting the surrender over to General Von Senger und Etterlin, XIV Panzerkorps commanding general who acted as General Heinrich von Vietinghoff's representative.
111-SC-208525

An Army in captivity. The massive prisoner camp at Brescia held thousands of prisoners of the German Fourteenth Army.
111-SC-210213

The Allied generals surround General Mark Clark, 15th Army Group's commanding officer, during a visit to Milan after the Armistice had been signed.
111-SC-208114

Chapter Six

Clearing the final pockets of resistance

AS BRITISH, CANADIAN, FRENCH AND AMERICAN troops pulled up along the banks of the River Elbe and River Mulde, the race was on to be the first to meet the Russians. Although Eisenhower had withdrawn his bridgeheads behind the rivers, as April drew to a close dozens of patrols scouted the far bank in the hope of meeting their Allies. A patrol from the 69th Infantry Division won the race, meeting a lone Russian horseman in the village of Leckwitz on the morning of the 25th and by the end of the day several other patrols had made contact. The German forces had been split in two. The following day Major-General Emil Reinhardt met Major-General Vladimir Rusakov of the Russian 58th Guards Division at Torgau in the first of many link-up ceremonies.

While 12 Army Group's spread out to quell pockets of resistance bypassed during the pursuit to the Elbe, 21 Army Group drove north and First Canadian Army reached the North Sea coast on 16 April, isolating German troops in Holland. A local cease-fire enabled airdrops to bring food in to help the starving population, the start of a massive Allied relief effort across war-torn Europe.

Meanwhile, Second British Army fought its way through Hamburg and Bremen, heading northeast and crossed the Elbe on 29 April. Three days later Montgomery's troops had reached Luebeck and Wismar on the Baltic coast, isolating enemy forces in the Jutland peninsula from the rest of Germany.

To the south 6th Army Group was engaged in a race to reach the Austrian mountains before German troops devoted to their Fuehrer could turn the area into a fortress known as the 'National Redoubt'. Seventh Army crossed the Austrian border on 28 April and two days later captured Munich, liberating nearby Dachau concentration camp, one of the largest of the Death Camps entered by Allied troops. A rapid advance through Austria quelled any chances of a last-stand and by 4 May Berchtesgaden, Hitler's command post in the National Redoubt, had been captured. Hitler did not try to join his men in the Alps, preferring to commit suicide in his Berlin bunker as Russian troops closed in from every side. Before long all the passes into the Alps had been taken, securing the area. Meanwhile, General Devers' troops roamed freely and as Third Army entered Czechoslovakia on 4 May, Seventh Army patrols met Fifth US Army patrols on the Italian frontier as they moved north from the Po River. The end was in sight.

As US troops drive south towards the Alps, an endless column of prisoners heads into captivity.

British armour moving up to support the British and Canadian advance across the north of Germany.

The Nazis promise to defend their National Redoubt in the Alps was dashed by 6th Army Group's lightning advance through Bavaria and Austria. These soldiers of 44th Division have just finished clearing pockets of resistance in the wooded foothills of the Tyrolean Alps.
111-SC-207672

As US troops raced across Germany and into Austria, news of President Roosevelt's death saddened every American servicemen. 103rd *Cactus* Division heard the news as it moved into the Austrian Alps; the Stars and Stripes hangs at half-mast outside 411th Regiment's command post in the village of Cries.
111-SC-206034

First Army's drive in the north reached the Baltic Sea on 3 May, cutting off German forces in the north. This tank of the *Lucky* 7th Armoured Division dips its tracks in the sea at Rehna to mark the occasion.
111-SC-206584

Meanwhile, in the south Seventh Army drove deep into southern Germany, passing through Bavaria on its way to the Austrian Alps. Wehrmacht and Luftwaffe prisoners are marched through the streets of Munich as tanks roll by while GIs of the 42nd *Rainbow* Division cling on.
111-SC-207621

Fighting intensified as Seventh Army entered Austria but the weight of armour and infantry quickly overwhelmed pockets of resistance. These men of 103rd Division have run into a group of fanatical Nazis in the town of Auland during the advance towards Innsbruck.
111-SC-269200

Third Army entered Czechoslovakia at the end of April and on 4 May met Fifth Army troops on the Italian frontier, linking the Italian and European theatres for the first time. These local girls have turned out in traditional dress to meet 97th *Trident* Division and 16th Armoured Division as they cleared Pilsen; the famous beer and munitions city was the deepest American penetration into Czechoslovakia.
111-SC-206401

Ninth US Army made the first contact with Soviet patrols along the Elbe on 30 April, having withdrawn behind the river. This soldier of 83rd Division is trying to charm a Russian soldier at Cobbelsdorf.
111-SC-207700

General Simpson, and Major-General Ray McLain, the only National Guardsman to command a corps, shows publisher Amon Carter, Brigadier-General Tauser of the War Office and undersecretary for war Robert Patterson, a temporary bridge over the Elbe. The bridge has been named after the new American President, Harry Truman. 83rd Division were living up to their nicknames, the *Thunderbolts*, crossing the Elbe on 13 April and was ready to advance on Berlin before Eisenhower ordered his men back behind the river.
111-SC-206604

Paratroopers of 6th British Airborne Division, veterans of D-Day and Operation Varsity, met Russian troops east of Wismar following Second Army's drive to the Baltic coast. 111-SC-206368

The Army photographers were kept busy as the war came to close, recording a host of important ceremonies for posterity. American, British, Canadian and Russian photographers gathered at Wismar for their own impromptu gathering. 111-SC-205370

General Walton Walker, XX Corps commanding general, hosted one of the first official ceremonies on Third Army's front. He met General Birokoff and the staff of the Fourth Russian Army on the Enns River in Austria.
111-SC-204674

On 30 April Adolf Hitler and his new wife Eva Braun committed suicide in the Fuehrer's Bunker as Russians troops roamed through the streets of Berlin. These soldiers heard the news while on leave in Paris and they are eagerly reading the report in a special edition of the US Army newspaper, Stars and Stripes. 111-SC-204386

Some German soldiers were determined to fight on even though their Fuehrer was dead. 103rd Division encountered a group of fanatical SS students in Scharnitz as Seventh Army drove into the heart of the Austrian Alps. 111-SC-205922

Task Force 409, comprising infantry mounted on tanks of the 781st Tank Battalion and tank destroyers of 614th Tank Destroyer Battalion, led VI Corps' drive through Innsbruck and reached the Brenner Pass on 4 May, closing the Alps off to German troops heading towards the National Redoubt. 111-SC-205923

Only a fraction of those expected to gather in the National Redoubt actually reached the Alps due to Seventh Army's rapid advance. This group of a thousand officers and men had gathered in the mountains above Innsbruck ready to make a last stand but quickly decided that their cause was lost and surrendered to Task Force 409 on 2 May. 111-SC-205294

3rd Division met this group of German soldiers on the road to Berchtesgaden, Hitler's retreat in the heart of the Alps. They have decided against making a last stand and appear relieved that their war is over.
111-SC-204343

GIs of 30th Infantry Regiment roll into Berchtesgaden village mounted on a tank; there is no sign of the rumoured last stand by SS troops in the mountains beyond. 111-SC-204385

Major-General John Iron Mike O'Daniel's 3rd Division reached Hitler's hilltop retreat on 4 May; German troops had set fire to the building before American troops could stop them. 111-SC-204344

Organising the surrender of hundreds of thousands of soldiers scattered across Europe was a delicate and complicated progress. The first stage was to arrange Armistices with local commanders to prevent unnecessary fighting. Generals' Haislip, Patch and Devers are checking the surrender document before handing them over to General Foertsch, the First German Army's Commander and personal representative of Field Marshal von Kesselring, leader of Army Group G.   111-SC-208235

The German surrender delegation arrives at Field Marshal Montgomery's headquarters at Lüneburg

130

On 5 May General Admiral Hans von Friedburg visited Eisenhower's headquarters on behalf of Hitler's successor, Admiral Karl Doenitz, in the hope of securing separate terms with the Allies. Eisenhower rejected the offer, the Russians had to be involved in the unconditional surrender.
III-SC-205948

Air Chief Marshal Sir Arthur Tedder, the Supreme Deputy Commander, inspects a Russian guard of honour at Tempelhof Airfield in Berlin. Tedder had flown to the German capital on 7 May to draw up surrender terms with the Russian Chief of Staff.
111-SC-206281

Field Marshal Wilhem Keitel signs the ratified surrender terms for the German Army at the Russian headquarters in Berlin; a precursor to signing the unconditional surrender terms.
111-SC-206292

Tedder signs the surrender terms on behalf of the Western Allied forces. 111-SC-206297

Field Marshal Georgi Zhukov, Deputy Commander of the Soviet Armed Forces, countersigns the document.
111-SC-206298

The final stage of the surrender process took place at SHAEF's headquarters in Rheims, France. This is the sombre moment in Eisenhower's war room as each party signs the papers, bringing six years of war in Europe to an end. 111-SC-205954

As the Allied press stand by, General Gustav Jodl, Hitler's Chief of Staff, signs the surrender terms. His aide Major Willem Oxenius, on the left, and General Admiral Hans von Friedeburg, commander in chief of the German Navy, look on gloomily as the proceedings get under way. 111-SC-204260

After a difficult eleven-month campaign General Dwight D Eisenhower has achieved his final objective, the defeat of Nazi Germany. The look on his face says it all.
111-SC-204256

Chapter Seven

Victory in Europe

BY THE END OF APRIL 1945 the thousand year Third Reich was finished. The German Armies had been scattered by the Allies, large areas of their home land had been occupied and their Führer was dead. Attempts by Admiral Karl Doenitz, Hitler's successor, to negotiate surrender terms with the Western Allies on 7 May was rejected and later that day his representative, General Alfred Jodl, was authorised to surrender on all fronts. The war in Europe formally came to an end on 8 May, a triumph of Allied strategy and tactics supported by a huge armaments industry.

As the news spread spontaneous celebrations broke out across the world as thousands of prisoners flooded into makeshift compounds across Germany. One by one Hitler's military and political leaders were rounded up and prepared for forthcoming trials relating to their war crimes. Although the Nazi regime had collapsed it would take years to rebuild the devastated cities and towns across Europe. Thousands of soldiers and civilians had been killed and injured; many more were homeless or refugees. As the Allied forces divided Germany into occupation zones the long process of rebuilding would begin.

As the soldiers looked forward to returning home after years of separation from their families, the Allied High Command still had to defeat Japan and many veterans of the campaigns in Europe had the prospect of moving to the Pacific theatre. Before news of Japan's unconditional surrender was approved, the Emperor had captitulated after two atomic bombs had been detonated over Hiroshima and Nagasaki. After six long years World War Two was over.

Officers of the Highland Division accept the German surrender at Bremerhaven. A major of the Black Watch checks that a surrendered Walther pistol is unloaded.

When Third Army began processing their haul of prisoners in the Passau area, Wehrmacht soldiers accused these ten SS soldiers of taking part in a massacre of American troops at Malmedy in the Ardennes in December 1944. The group were also charged with executing dozens of slave labourers. The Allies devoted a huge amount of resources to rounding up and putting to trial war criminals culminating in the prosecution of senior Nazi officers and politicians at the Nuremberg War Trials.

111-SC-341511

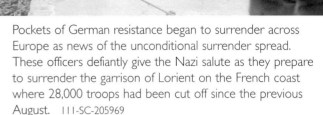

Pockets of German resistance began to surrender across Europe as news of the unconditional surrender spread. These officers defiantly give the Nazi salute as they prepare to surrender the garrison of Lorient on the French coast where 28,000 troops had been cut off since the previous August.   111-SC-205969

Delicate negotiations were sometimes required to encourage groups of Germans to surrender. This SS Major and Lieutenant of the *Hassenstien* Division have come to 65th Division's headquarters to discuss terms with Major-General Stanley E. Reinhart. The blindfolds are for security purposes in case the talks fail; the American positions have to remain a secret.   111-SC-2064503

Field Marshal Gerd von Rundstedt, one of Hitler's top generals was 'hired and fired' on more than one occasion as the Führer's favours changed. He was appointed Supreme Commander on the Western front following Rommel's departure and removed from his post after the loss of Remagen Bridge. Here he is talking to Major-General Frank Milburn, 36th Division's leader, at XXI Corps headquarters in Weilheim.   111-SC-207632

Following Hitler's suicide, Field Marshal Herman Goering, was one of the Allies greatest catches. The Luftwaffe leader talks to Major-General John Dahlquist, 36th Division's commander, and his assistant, Brigadier-General Robert Stack at Kitzbuhel's Grand Hotel in Austria, a few days after Germany's surrender. Goering appeared at the Nuremberg trials and although he was found guilty and sentenced to death, he cheated the gallows by committing suicide.   111-SC-206580

This gun crew of 740th Field Artillery Battalion were about to fire this shell in support of Third Army's advance through Czechoslovakia when the order to cease-fire was given.
111-SC-206890

Germany's forces were scattered far and wide across Europe and it took several weeks to round up hundreds of thousands of men and their vehicles. This group of German tanks in Oslo, Norway, were handed over to British troops at the beginning of June.
111-SC-208071

42nd Rainbow Division encountered bitter fighting during Seventh Army's advance through southern Germany but nothing could prepare Major-General Henry J Collins and his men for the horrors at Dachau on the outskirts of Munich. On 29 April 30,000 inmates of one of the most notorious of the Nazi concentration camps was liberated. These GIs have to the stop prisoners leaving through the main gate due to a typhoid outbreak. 111-SC-206312

As the days passed, the true horror of the concentration camps unfolded. Thousands of inmates including, Jews, political prisoners, Jehovah's Witnesses, homosexuals and gypsies were worked to death or executed. 82nd *All American* Airborne Division liberated Woebling Camp in Ninth Army's area and despite attempts to administer medical aid, some inmates were beyond help.
111-SC-206379

Emotions ran high as the camps were entered and some inmates exacted their revenge on their guards before they could be stopped. This man's tears sum up the relief of thousands liberated by the Allies.
111-SC-206390

On 8 May 1945 news that the war in Europe had come to an end spread around the world. Outside Paris Opera House soldiers and civilians climb above the gathering crowds to celebrate. 111-205959

London, 8 May, V-E or Victory in Europe night and after five and a half years of blackout, the Houses of Parliament and Big Ben are lit up. Street parties continued throughout the night as everyone looked forward to peace in Europe. 111-SC-206422

Thousands of civilians mingle with servicemen around Nelson's Column in Trafalgar Square to participate in the Victory Parade on 8 May. The posters read 'Victory over Germany 1945 – Give thanks by saving', a reference to War Bonds, a Government savings scheme designed to boost the war effort.

VICTORY OVER GERMANY 1945 GIVE THANKS BY SAVING

Prime Minister Winston Churchill welcomes Eisenhower to the London Guild Hall just before he was given the freedom of the city.
111-SC-207715

Corporals Gahlen Brown and Ted Perfitt play the tune 'Oh how I hate to get up in the morning' for the last time as these soldiers wait to be taken to the embarkation ports. The graffiti on the German train says it all.
111-SC-207609

After eleven months in action and three months occupation duty in Germany this shipload of GIs are looking forward to going home. These veterans of the 30th *Old Hickory* Division had fought their way from Normandy across France and deep into the heart of Germany. Now it is time to return to the States on the Queen Mary.
111-SC-210468

These men of the 1st and 9th Infantry Divisions were veterans of the campaigns in North Africa, Sicily, France, Belgium and Germany and among the first group to head home. The US Army's Green Project sent home 20,000 men a month by air.
111-SC-208269

It would take years before Germany recovered from the ruin and devastation brought upon their country by war. As the Luftwaffe's power declined, the Allied bombing campaign had intensified, decimating industry and housing alike. This suburb of Bremen was raised to the ground.
111-SC-210501

Thousands of men would never go home. Henri-Chapelle Cemetery in Belgium was one of the largest American War Cemeteries in Europe.   111-SC-1999968